Contents

What is fruit?

Fruit is a part of a plant that you can eat. Fruit usually contains seeds that can grow into new plants.

There are many different kinds of fruit, such as strawberries, oranges, bananas, grapes and tomatoes.

Vic Parker

QED Publishing

First published in the UK in 2009 by
QED Publishing
A Quarto Group company
226 City Road
London EC1V 2TT

www.qed-publishing.co.uk

A catalogue record for this book is available from the British Library.

ISBN 978 1 84835 247 6

Author Vic Parker
Consultant Angela Royston
Project Editor Eve Marleau
Designer Kim Hall
Illustrator Mike Byrne

Publisher Steve Evans
Creative Director Zeta Davies
Managing Editor Amanda Askew

Printed and bound in China

Picture credits
(t=top, b=bottom, l=left, r=right, c=centre, fc=front cover)

Alamy 5t Blickwinkel, 12cl Stuart Forster, 14cl Per Karlsson – BKWine.com

Corbis 14b Jack K Clark

Photolibrary 9b Foodpix, 12b Douglas Peebles, 13c Raymond Forbes, 19bl AJJ Estudi

Rex Features 13t Sipa Press

Shutterstock 4tl Eric Gevaert, 4tc Andrjuss, 4tr Andrjuss,4bl Zloneg, 4br Valentyn Volkov, 5c Vondelmol, 5b Ricardo Manuel Silva de Sousa, 6l Zloneg, 6r Eric Gevaert, 6–7 Martine Oger, 7tl Valentyn Volkov, 7tr Andrjuss, 7c Whaldener Endo, 7bl Elena Schweitzer, 7br Andrjuss, 8t Antonio Munoz Palomares, 8bl Khomulo Anna, 8bc, Junial Enterprises, 8br Branislav Senic, 9t Matka Wariatka, 11tl Serp, 11tr Stephen Aaron Rees, 11t (orange) Valentyn Volkov, 11c (banana) Andrjuss, 11c (kiwi) Tihis, 11c (strawberries) Marek Mnich, 11bl (apple) Bliznetsov, 11bl (banana) Yasonya, 11bc Victor Burnside, 11br Yasonya, 12t Andrjuss, 12cr Alex Kuzovlev, 13b Christopher Elwell, 14t Andrjuss, 14cr Riekephotos, 15t Carolina K Smith, 15cl Morgan Lane Photography, 15cr Ultimathule, 15bl Lepas, 15br Konstantynov, 16 Eric Gevaert, 17t Stephen Aaron Rees, 17b Serp, 18t Zloneg, 18c Paul Prescott, 18b Christopher Elwell, 19t Guy Erwood, 19c eAlisa, 19brt Yellowj, 19brb Oliver Hoffmann

Words in **bold** are explained in the glossary on page 22.

You will need

- Young blueberry plant
- 30-cm or 40-cm pot
- Ericaceous, or acidic, **compost** and **fertilizer**
- Watering can

Grow a... blueberry plant

1. At any time of year, plant your blueberry plant into a 30-cm or 40-cm pot filled with ericaceous compost. Water it well with rainwater. Keep the soil damp.
2. In the spring, when the leaves have all opened, ask an adult to help you feed your plant with ericaceous fertilizer.
3. By late spring, your bush will be covered with white flowers. Keep watering it and watch for green fruits to appear that will ripen into juicy blueberries.

Fruit grows from plants. Most fruits grow on trees or bushes. The seeds of these plants are usually found inside the fruit.

⇨A pomegranate has hundreds of seeds inside.

Where are different fruits grown?

Different types of fruit are grown all over the world.

Each type of fruit needs the right conditions to make it grow. Some fruits need lots of water. Others grow well in very hot, dry weather.

North America

South America

Tomatoes grow well in warm weather. A lot of tomatoes are grown in Mexico and the United States of America.

Strawberries grow well in warm, dry weather. Many strawberries are grown in North America.

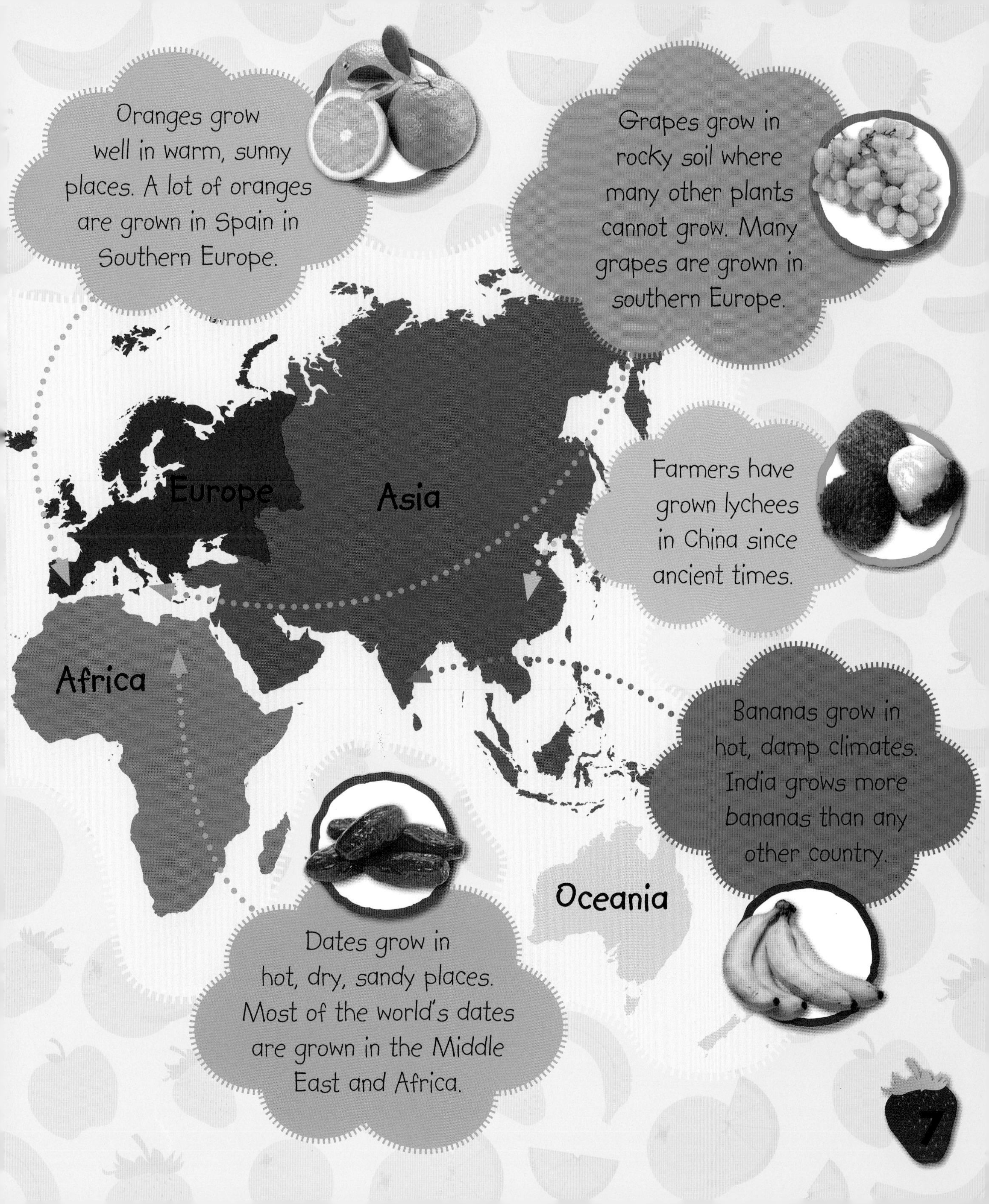
Oranges grow well in warm, sunny places. A lot of oranges are grown in Spain in Southern Europe.
Grapes grow in rocky soil where many other plants cannot grow. Many grapes are grown in southern Europe.
Europe
Asia
Africa
Farmers have grown lychees in China since ancient times.
Bananas grow in hot, damp climates. India grows more bananas than any other country.
Oceania
Dates grow in hot, dry, sandy places. Most of the world's dates are grown in the Middle East and Africa.

How do we eat fruit?

Fruit can be eaten at all times of the day. You can have it fresh, frozen, dried, canned or as juice.

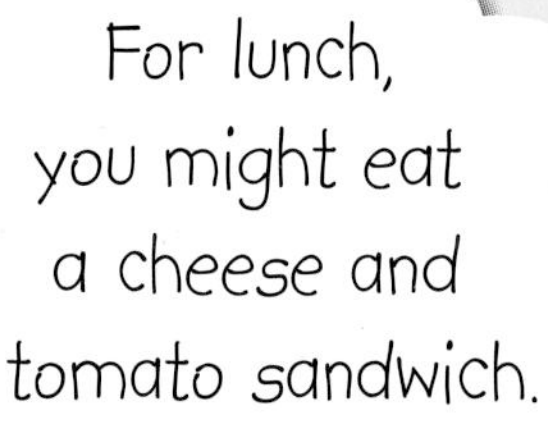

For lunch, you might eat a cheese and tomato sandwich.

At breakfast, you can add fresh fruit, such as berries, or dried fruit, such as raisins, to yoghurt or cereal.

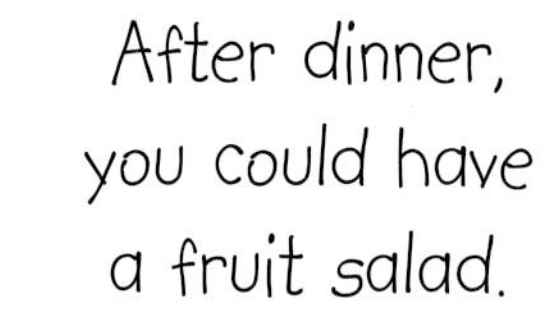

After dinner, you could have a fruit salad.

You will need

- 6 ice cubes
- 4 strawberries
- 1 banana, chopped
- 2 scoops of mango ice cream
- 150 ml milk
- Blender
- Glass

Make a... smoothie

1. Crush the ice in the blender. Blend for two minutes.
2. Add the other ingredients and blend for about 40 seconds until the mixture is smooth.
3. Pour it into a glass and drink.

Some fruits need peeling before you eat them, such as oranges. You can eat many other fruits with their skins on, such as plums and apples. Always wash these fruits before eating.

⇧ Fruit can be made into jams, smoothies and other foods.

Why does your body need fruit?

Fresh fruit contains vitamins, minerals and *fibre*, **which are good for your body.**

Most fruits contain fibre, which your body needs to help it get rid of waste food.

Some fruits, such as bananas, contain iron, which helps to keep your blood healthy.

Fruits such as oranges contain Vitamin C, which is needed for your body to **absorb** iron from food.

Strawberries
Red fruits such as strawberries contain antioxidants, which help your body to fight off germs.
Oranges
Fruits such as oranges are good for your eyes and skin.
Bananas
Yellow fruits such as bananas contain potassium, which is good for your **blood pressure**.
Kiwis
Green fruits such as kiwis are good for your **digestive system**.
Food news
To stay healthy, you should eat five portions of different fruit and vegetables every day.
1
2
3
4
5

How are bananas grown?

To grow bananas, farmers cut and plant shoots from the underground stems of banana plants.

1 Farmers plant banana shoots, which are called suckers. After 3–4 weeks, leaves begin to sprout.

2 After about two months, a large bud grows from the leaves. As the plant stem grows taller, this bud opens into groups of small flowers.

3 Six months after the shoot was planted, the flowers turn into bananas. Each group, or hand, has 10–20 bananas in it.

4 After nine months, when the bananas are still green, farmers cut them from the plants.

They are washed, put into boxes and kept cold so they don't ripen. They are then sent to shops and factories, where the temperature makes the bananas ripen and turn yellow.

5

You will need

- 1 scoop of frozen yoghurt
- 1 banana
- 50 g fruit, such as strawberries
- Knife
- Bowl

Make a... banana split

1. Place the frozen yoghurt into a bowl.
2. Cut the banana lengthwise and place the two pieces either side of the frozen yoghurt.
3. Sprinkle with strawberries and serve.

How are grapes grown?

Grapes are grown from small cuttings, or pieces, that growers take from grapevines.

1 The cuttings are planted in soil. They grow for about three years before they produce grapes.

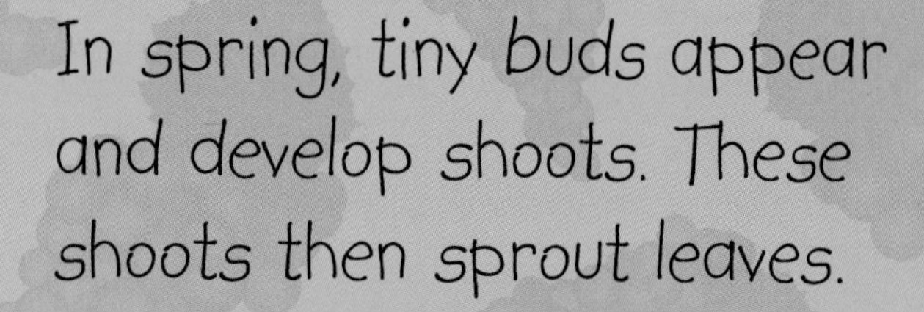

In spring, tiny buds appear and develop shoots. These shoots then sprout leaves.

2

3 About two months after the first buds appear, small groups of flowers grow on the shoots. These flowers turn into grapes.

4 In large **vineyards**, grapes are **harvested** by machines that look like tractors. They pull the clusters of grapes from the vines.

5 Grapevines lose their leaves in autumn and are pruned, or cut, in winter. Some grapevines can live for about 50 years.

6 Some of these grapes are sold fresh in shops. Others are made into grape juice and wine.

Grow some strawberries

You will need

- Strawberry pot
- Compost
- Some pieces of broken crockery or plant pot
- Strawberry plant for each hole in the strawberry pot
- Watering can

In spring, place the broken crockery in the strawberry pot. Fill it with compost up to the first holes in the pot.

Push a strawberry plant through each of the holes. Fill the pot with compost to the next level of holes.

Continue planting until you reach the top of the strawberry pot. Place the pot in a sunny position and water the plants regularly.

After about two months, small, white flowers will bloom on your plants, then the strawberries will grow. When the strawberries are ripe and juicy, pick them.

Food news

Strawberries are the only fruit that has its seeds on the outside.

Tomatoes

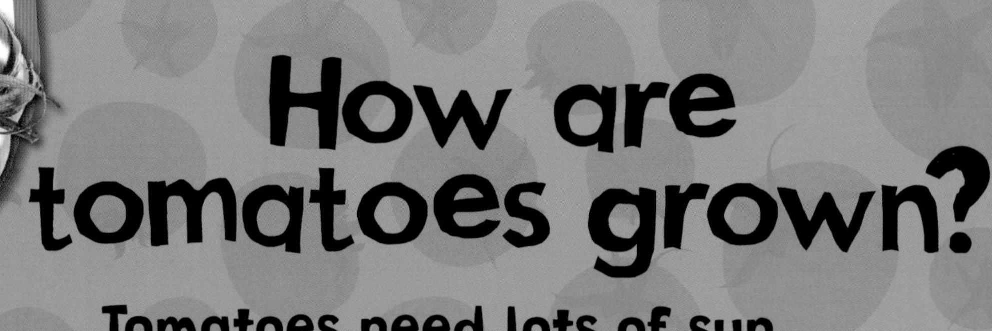

How are tomatoes grown?

Tomatoes need lots of sun to grow. They can be grown indoors and outdoors.

1

In warm places, farmers sow, or plant, tomato seeds in soil outdoors. In cooler places, farmers sow tomato seeds in pots inside warm **greenhouses**.

2

As the seedlings grow, they need plenty of water. Some farmers also feed them with fertilizer to help the plants to grow big and strong.

As the plants shoot up, they are tied to canes, so they don't flop over. Small bunches of yellow flowers appear. These drop off, leaving little green tomatoes behind.

The fruits are usually harvested when they are unripe and still green. This is so the tomatoes stay fresh for longer on their way to shops and factories.

Eat a... tomato

Eat a big beefsteak tomato, then eat a tiny cherry tomato – see how different they taste.

★ Ask an adult ★

Always ask an adult to help you make the recipe and get all the ingredients and equipment ready. Remember to wash your hands before you start.

Make fruity flapjacks

These tasty biscuits are packed with fruit.

You will need

- 150 g oats
- 50 g sugar
- 50 g butter or margarine, plus extra for greasing
- 2 tbsp of golden syrup
- 75 g dried fruit (such as raisins or apricots)
- Saucepan
- Wooden spoon
- Shallow baking tin
- Greaseproof paper
- Wire rack
- Knife

1 Ask an adult to preheat the oven to 200°C/400°F/Gas 6.

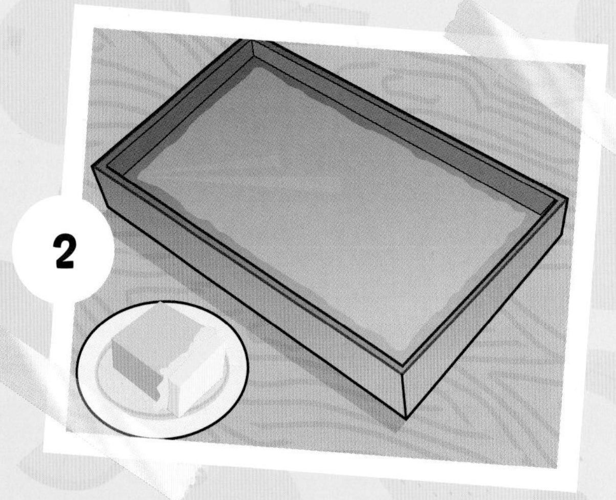

2 Grease the baking tin with butter and line with greaseproof paper.

3 Ask an adult to melt the syrup, sugar and butter or margarine in a saucepan. Stir in the oats.

4

Pour half of the mixture into the baking tin. Arrange the dried fruit over the oats.

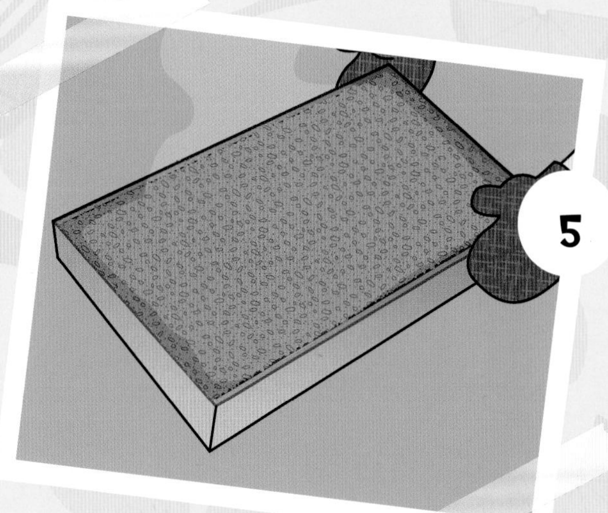

5

Pour the remaining mixture over the dried fruit. Bake it for 20 minutes until it is lightly browned.

6

Ask an adult to cut the flapjack into portions in the baking tin while it is still hot. Then put the pieces on a wire rack to cool.

Glossary

Absorb
To take something in.

Blood pressure
A measure of how easily your blood is flowing through your body.

Compost
Rotting plant material that is full of goodness. It is added to soil to improve its quality.

Digestive system
All the parts of your body that are involved in breaking down and using food, and getting rid of waste products.

Fertilizer
A substance that is spread on land or given to plants to make them grow well.

Fibre
A part of plants that your body can't digest. As fibre moves through your body, it soaks up water and makes it easier to get rid of waste food.

Greenhouse
A glass building where plants that need a lot of light are grown.

Harvest
To gather, or collect, crops from the field.

Vineyard
A piece of land on which lots of grapevines are grown.

Notes for parents and teachers

- Show the children a variety of food and pick out the pieces of fresh fruit. Discuss each fruit's size, shape, colour and texture.

- Look at supermarket labels and packaging to see which countries different fruits come from. Look at a map or globe and identify the places that these fruits come from.

- Find photographs of what different fruits look like when they are growing. Choose one to draw and then label the different parts of the plant (roots, stem, branches, leaves and fruit).

- Talk about how we eat different kinds of fresh fruit. Can we eat the skin? Do we need to peel it? Should we eat the seeds? Show other forms that the fruit comes in, such as dried, tinned and frozen.

- Discuss why our bodies need fruit to stay healthy. Explain how much fruit we should eat each day and why it's best to eat different kinds.

- Talk about how we might use different types of fruit in cooking. Make an international fruit cookbook with recipes and pictures from around the world.

Index